CONTENTS

P9-DWT-433

Words in the glossary appear in **bold** type the first time they are used in the text.

SO CUTE... AND DEADLY!

Seals are cute creatures, especially if you've ever seen them playing in the water. But make no mistake—these **mammals** can be tough. They're carnivores, which means they eat meat. They have the sharp teeth to prove it.

There are 32 species, or kinds, of seals. One stands out as the most dangerous: the leopard seal. While most seals eat fish and some shellfish, leopard seals are hungry for bigger prey. While you should never get too close to this cold-water creature, you should read on to learn all about it!

THE DANGEROUS DETAILS

Leopard seals are apex predators. That means they're at the top of their food chain.

4

CUTEST ANIMALS...
THAT COULD **KILL** YOU!

ALARMING

LEOPARD SEALS

 Gareth Stevens
PUBLISHING

BY ELEANOR SNYDER

Please visit our website, www.garethstevens.com. For a free color catalog of all our high-quality books, call toll free 1-800-542-2595 or fax 1-877-542-2596.

Library of Congress Cataloging-in-Publication Data

Names: Snyder, Eleanor, author.
Title: Alarming leopard seals / Eleanor Snyder.
Description: New York : Gareth Stevens Publishing, [2017] | Series: Cutest
  animals . . . that could kill you! | Includes bibliographical references
  and index.
Identifiers: LCCN 2015046971 | ISBN 9781482449150 (pbk.) | ISBN 9781482449099 (library bound) |
ISBN 9781482448979 (6 pack)
Subjects: LCSH: Leopard seal–Juvenile literature.
Classification: LCC QL737.P64 S627 2017 | DDC 599.79/6–dc23
LC record available at http://lccn.loc.gov/2015046971

First Edition

Published in 2017 by
Gareth Stevens Publishing
111 East 14th Street, Suite 349
New York, NY 10003

Copyright © 2017 Gareth Stevens Publishing

Designer: Sarah Liddell
Editor: Therese Shea

Photo credits: Cover, p. 1 Danita Delimont/Gallo Images/Getty Images; wood texture used throughout Imageman/Shutterstock.com; slash texture used throughout d1sk/Shutterstock.com; p. 5 Mogens Trolle/Shutterstock.com; p. 6 Eric Isselee/Shutterstock.com; p. 7 Wolfgang Kaehler/Contributor/LightRocket/Getty Images; p. 9 (main) Matt Berger/Shutterstock.com; p. 9 (map) AridOcean/Shutterstock.com; pp. 11, 15, 19 Paul Nicklen/National Geographic/Getty Images; p. 13 Kansas City Star/Contributor/Tribune News Service/Getty Images; p. 16 Jan Martin Will/Shutterstock.com;
p. 17 Paul Nicklen/Contributor/National Geographic/Getty Images; p. 21 Barcroft/Contributor/Barcroft Media/Getty Images.

CPSIA compliance information: Batch #CS16GS: For further information contact Gareth Stevens, New York, New York at 1-800-542-2595.

LIKE A LEOPARD?

If you ever saw a leopard seal racing through the water, you'd call it beautiful. It has a narrow body that moves gracefully through the water. It can be quite heavy, though. Leopard seals can weigh as much as 840 pounds (381 kg). They can be up to 12 feet (3.7 m) long, too.

Leopard seals have a gray coat covered in black spots. That's how they got their name—from the black-spotted wild cat called the leopard. The leopard seal shares something else with the big cat. Both are fearsome!

LEOPARD

THE DANGEROUS DETAILS

Female leopard seals are
larger than males.

LOOKING FOR LEOPARD SEALS

Leopard seals are found in very cold waters near Antarctica. They've also been spotted near South Africa, southern Australia, and around New Zealand and other islands in the Southern **Hemisphere**.

Leopard seals, like other seals, spend time on land as well as in the water. Adults are often found on **pack ice**. They don't move very well on land, however. They're much, much quicker in the water, thanks to the power they get from their large **flippers**.

8

LEOPARD SEALS SPOTTED!

SUBANTARCTIC ISLANDS

AFRICA

SOUTH AMERICA

ANTARCTICA

AUSTRALIA

— WHERE LEOPARD SEALS LIVE

YOUNGER LEOPARD SEALS ARE OFTEN FOUND AROUND SUBANTARCTIC ISLANDS. THESE ARE ISLANDS NORTH OF ANTARCTICA.

9

BORN FOR THE WATER

The leopard seal's body is perfect for its home. It has a layer of blubber, or fat, that keeps it warm in really cold waters. Its **nostrils** are located on top of its **snout**, helping to keep water out as it swims along the surface. When a leopard seal dives, its nostrils close.

While some seals can remain underwater for as long as 70 minutes, the leopard seal can't. It usually dives for no longer than 15 minutes. Then, it has to come back up to breathe air.

WHEN LEOPARD SEALS EAT IN WATER, SPECIAL BODY PARTS WORK TO KEEP THEM FROM BREATHING IN WATER.

11

WHAT LOOKS TASTY?

Leopard seals have powerful **jaws** and long teeth. When they open their mouth, you can see their large **canines**. They also have special body parts on each side of their jaws that help them **filter** tiny sea creatures called krill from the water. Krill are easy prey to catch. Leopard seals also eat fish and **cephalopods** (SEH-fuh-luh-pahdz).

Leopard seals are the only seals that eat warm-blooded prey. This includes other seals and penguins. They can catch these prey animals in pretty sneaky ways!

THE LEOPARD SEAL DIET

- 30% OTHER SEALS
- 10% FISH AND CEPHALOPODS
- 45% KRILL
- 10% PENGUINS
- 5% OTHER

ADAPTATIONS LIKE THESE POINTED TEETH HELP LEOPARD SEALS CATCH AND EAT THEIR PREY.

13

SNEAK ATTACK!

Leopard seals are known for hiding under the ice. You don't want to play hide-and-seek with these mammals, though. They're waiting for birds, seals, and penguins to enter the water. Those animals are just looking for a bite to eat, too. Instead, they sometimes leap right into the large mouth of a leopard seal!

Leopard seals can also swim faster than some of their prey. At times, they're so fast they jump out of the water to catch prey on the edge of the ice.

THE DANGEROUS DETAILS

Seabirds resting on the water are easy snacks for leopard seals. The seals come from below and—SNAP!

PENGUINS HAVE BEEN KNOWN TO WAIT FOR OTHER PENGUINS TO ENTER THE WATER TO SEE IF IT'S SAFE FROM PREDATORS SUCH AS LEOPARD SEALS.

15

TOOTHY TERRORS

The leopard seal has teeth for biting, but not chewing. It can just swallow smaller animals. However, for bigger animals such as penguins, the seal gets more **vicious**. In order to break the animal into bite-size pieces, the leopard seal shakes its prey until it's torn apart. Yuck! That's not cute at all!

Leopard seals are also scavengers. That means they eat the rotting meat of dead animals. Leopard seals are known to eat whale meat they find.

LITTLE LEOPARD SEALS

Leopard seals are solitary creatures. That means they live and hunt alone. However, they come up on ice each year in November or December to find a **mate**.

About 11 months later, the mother leopard seal gives birth to a baby called a pup. The seal pup may weigh 70 pounds (32 kg)! It drinks its mother's milk for about a month. It gains weight fast to grow strong enough to go off by itself and hunt its own food.

THE DANGEROUS DETAILS

Leopard seals have been known to live as long as 25 years in the wild. However, they usually live only about 15 years.

NOT MUCH IS KNOWN ABOUT HOW A LEOPARD SEAL PUP GROWS. PUPS ARE RARELY SEEN IN THE WILD.

STAY AWAY!

As if leopard seals aren't scary enough, they've been known to attack people, too. Scientists working in Antarctica have been bitten and even dragged underwater by leopard seals. The creatures probably mistook the people for prey. Usually, leopard seals try to stay away from people.

Still, events like this are a great reminder that most wild animals are just that—wild. No matter how cute they look or act, they must be respected and left alone.

THE DANGEROUS DETAILS

It's thought there are 200,000 to 400,000 leopard seals around the world.

GLOSSARY

adaptation: a change in a type of animal that makes it better able to live in its surroundings

canine: a long, pointed tooth near the front of the mouth

cephalopod: a marine animal that has arms around the front of its head and a sac containing ink, including squids and octopuses

filter: to collect bits from a liquid passing through

flipper: a wide, flat "arm" used for swimming

hemisphere: one-half of Earth

jaw: one of the bones that hold the teeth and make up the mouth

mammal: a warm-blooded animal that has a backbone and hair, breathes air, and feeds milk to its young

mate: one of two animals that come together to produce babies

nostril: an opening in the nose through which an animal breathes

pack ice: floating ice that has formed into a solid mass over a wide area

snout: an animal's nose and mouth

vicious: dangerous and intending to do harm by fighting

FOR MORE INFORMATION

BOOKS

Barraclough, Susan, ed. *Sharks & Other Creatures of the Deep.* New York, NY: Sandy Creek, 2007.

Sexton, Colleen. *Seals.* Minneapolis, MN: Bellwether Media, 2007.

Tylers, Michael. *Predators of South America and Antarctica.* New York, NY: Cavendish Square Publishing, 2015.

WEBSITES

Leopard Seal
animals.nationalgeographic.com/animals/mammals/leopard-seal/
Find out more about this fierce predator.

Leopard Seals
www.afsc.noaa.gov/nmml/education/pinnipeds/leopard.php#live
See if your questions about leopard seals are answered on this site.

Publisher's note to educators and parents: Our editors have carefully reviewed these websites to ensure that they are suitable for students. Many websites change frequently, however, and we cannot guarantee that a site's future contents will continue to meet our high standards of quality and educational value. Be advised that students should be closely supervised whenever they access the Internet.

INDEX